MAORI

A VISITOR'S GUIDE

PAORA WALKER

PHOTOGRAPHY BY JAMES HEREMAIA

REED

REED PUBLISHING (NZ) LTD
TE KARUHI TĀ TĀPUI O REED (AOTEAROA)

Established in 1907, Reed is New Zealand's largest
book publisher, with over 600 titles in print.

www.reed.co.nz

Published by Reed Books, a division of Reed Publishing (NZ) Ltd, 39 Rawene Rd, Birkenhead,
Auckland. Associated companies, branches and representatives throughout the world.

Published by Reed Books

National Library of New Zealand Cataloguing-in-Publication Data

Walker, Paora.
Māori : a visitor's guide / by Paora Walker ; photographs by
James Heremaia.
ISBN 978-0-7900-1101-1
1. Maori (New Zealand people)—Social life and customs. 2. Maori
(New Zealand people)—Material culture.[1. Tangata whenua.
2. Tikanga.] I. Heremaia, James. II. Title.
305.899442—dc 22

ISBN-13 978 07900 1101 1
ISBN-10 0 7900 1101 8

All photographs are by James Heremaia except the following: Archives New Zealand Te Whare
Tohu Tuhituhinga o Aotearoa (page 38) Garry Brandon (6, 54, 68, 70); Hawke's Bay Inc. (26);
Graham Hooper (76); Robert Key (9,29,53); Holge Leue (78,82); Te Wānanga o Aotearoa (18); Te
Whakaata Māori/Māori Television (37).

Design: Suzanne Wesley
Cover images: James Heremaia
Printed in China by Nordica

CONTENTS

ACKNOWLEDGEMENTS

The author acknowledges with gratitude the supply of photographs and/or permission to photograph from the following individuals and organisations.

Te Wānanga o Aotearoa for the photos of the replica migration waka *Aotearoa One*, which is a wonderful floating classroom and vehicle for knowledge transfer.

The Māori Studies Department of the University of Auckland for permission to photograph their beautiful whare whakairo, Tāne-nui-a-Rangi.

Hawke's Bay Incorporated for the photo of the sign to the longest placename in the world.

Māori Television for the image of a Māori TV presenter.

Garry Brandon, Graham Hooper and Robert Key for photographs.

James Heremaia: Ka nui te mihi ki a koe e Hemi mō tōu tautoko ki te pukapuka nei, ā, mō ōu whakaahua ātaahua. Tēnā koe, e koro, te tohunga a te mahi whakaahua.

Ka nui te mihi ki a koutou katoa mō ōu koutou āwhina, tautoko hoki ki tēnei pukapuka.

INTRODUCTION

The inspiration for this book came from the publisher who felt that visitors to Aotearoa / New Zealand would be enriched by exposure to things Māori, and that it would be good for all concerned if those visitors could learn a little prior to their exposure – which is why I've entered the picture.

Now, as my friend Nick Theobald, co-writer and publisher of *Instant! Māori* (Writer & Writer Ltd, 2004), says, 'We're all tourists when it comes to the world of the Māori.' So this book is not only for overseas visitors, your genuine tourists, it's for all of us. Tātou. That's 'tar-toe'.

Cultural understanding leads to harmony. We're all in the same boat and harmony among the crew will enhance the voyage. As Pōtatau (the first Māori king) said at his coronation in 1858:

> There is only one eye of the needle through which must pass the white thread, the black thread, and the red thread.

In saying these words Pōtatau was echoing the proclamation of the first governor of New Zealand who, at the signing of the Treaty of Waitangi in 1840, said:

> We are all one people.

I was raised in the Pākehā world, starting my life in Urenui, a Taranaki village where one of the favourite winter school sports was the lunchtime rugby game of 'Maoris vs Pakehas'.

From very early on I was aware that one of my ancestors was a Māori woman whose portrait adorned a wall at my granny's house. At twenty-five I dived into researching my Māori whakapapa, genealogy. The research led me into another world which I barely knew existed. I had been to the pā, village, in Urenui, and one of the most colourful memories from my childhood is going to the welcome home to the ashes of Te Rangihiroa, Sir Peter Buck at Okoki pā, just north of Urenui in 1954.

However, during a four-year stint at Waikato University I often visited marae, tribal meeting grounds, and studied the Māori language and culture, and I eventually arrived at what, for me, was something of a revelation.

There were two very distinct worlds within New Zealand and, within one of those worlds, that of the Pākehā, there was an almost complete ignorance of the other, the Māori world. In order to survive, Māori had been forced to join the Pākehā world – move to the big smoke – which they increasingly did throughout the latter half of the twentieth century. Māori were actively encouraged to turn their backs on their culture, to not speak their language, to embrace the world of the Pākehā. How else were they to get on? Well, fortunately there were a good number of Māori who managed to get on *and* maintain their links with their culture. Which was just as well because they were needed to help their relations participate in the cultural renaissance of things Māori, which took hold in the 1970s and has gained momentum ever since.

For myself, the journey into the past and thereby into the present has been a wonderful, enlightening experience. I'm currently looking forward to seeing my ten-year-old son deliver his first whaikōrero, speech, on his school's upcoming marae visit.

I am not an expert in any of the areas I have written about in the following pages. However, my time at university taught me how to research and record, and I have sought out writings by acknowledged authorities on the various areas covered in this book. The goal is to provide you with a window, the view through which will motivate you to then open the door and enter the world of the Māori.

Nā reira, e aku tūpuna, mihi mai, karanga mai. Tukuna mai ōu koutou aroha ki ōu mokopuna e mahi ana ki tēnei taonga o te ao Māori.

Paora Walker
Auckland, 2007

MYTH

How was our world created? Māori account for it this way.

In the beginning was the kore, the nothingness or the potential for life, which lasted who knows how long as there was not even the concept of time. The kore became the pō, the night, which went through twelve stages before it finally became te ao mārama, the world of light. It is within the story of how the pō became te ao mārama that the description of the creation of our world and universe can be found.

The reason that the pō was so dark for so long was that Ranginui, the first male deity, lay with the first female deity Papatūānuku. Such was their regard for each other they could not bear to be parted. They produced many children. Exact numbers are uncertain – some say seventy and some say seventy-seven. These numbers do, however, indicate that the lovers lay together for quite some time.

Meanwhile the offspring who resided within the embrace of their parents became bored with their habitat, especially when some of them glimpsed light out through the armpit of one of their parents.

And so the children resolved to separate their parents in order that they might enter te ao mārama. The oldest brother, Tāne, lay on his back and forced his father to separate upwards from his lover Papatūānuku. Some say he broke off Rangi's arms in the process, while others believe that such were the frantic efforts of Rangi and Papa to stay together they lacerated each other's arms. However it happened, Rangi's blood stained the western skies where it is often still seen today, morning and evening. Papa's blood flowed to earth where it became red ochre clay, which is used in the adornment

Rangi's blood over Mt Taranaki.

of waka, canoes, and whare, houses.

This is how Ranginui came to be the sky father and Papatūānuku the earth mother. Their grief and sadness at being separated is still witnessed today. Rangi's tears fall in the form of rain and Papa's are manifested in mist which reaches up to enfold her estranged lover.

Of the seventy or so children, seven became awesome deities who formed, shaped and directed all the elements and physical makeup of the world and universe as we know it. These seven children were very competitive.

Papa's tears in the Hokianga. *Robert Key*

Tawhirimātea, whose realm was the winds and the elements, did not like the way his parents were separated. He flew into a rage and brought all his powers to bear on his brothers. Tāne, who went on to create the forests, birds of the sea and land, and then people, was felled by Tawhirimātea. Rongo, whose domain became that of plants cultivated by man, and Haumiatiketike, overseer of nature's foods, both hid underground. Tangaroa took refuge in the sea where he became ruler. Tūmatauenga, who became god of war, was so angry with the poor resistance offered by his brothers to Tawhirimātea that he decided to punish them. He caught and ate fish, progeny of Tangaroa; dug up and ate the plants of Rongo and Haumiatiketike; felled Tāne's trees and made tools and waka from them.

Another brother, Whiro, challenged the actions of all of the other six but he was eventually driven down into the underworld where he assumed the reign as god of evil.

The youngest of Rangi and Papa's children was Rūaumoko, and his brothers left him with his parents as he was very young and still being breastfed. As a consolation to both Rūaumoko and his parents, the brothers turned their mother over, thereby removing her pain at having to gaze upon her estranged lover, and they placed Rūaumoko deep in the earth below her and gave him fire with which he could keep his mother warm. Rūaumoko was furious at his treatment and, as the god of earthquakes, he is still venting his anger at the perpetrators of his fate.

Such a tumultuous beginning to our world.

RELIGION

The Māori concept of the spiritual and physical is one of total interdependence of the two worlds. In traditional times, and still on many occasions today, no action could be taken or even contemplated without the appropriate karakia, prayer, being recited to acknowledge the deities and to ensure success. There were atua, gods/ spirits, and taniwha, demons, everywhere and they had to be acknowledged and accorded respect. Failure to provide such acknowledgement and respect in the correct manner – as prescribed by the definitive laws of tapu – could result in disaster being visited upon the offenders.

The law of tapu, sacredness, and noa, non-sacred state, governed absolutely every facet of the Māori world. If the laws of tapu were breached then the mana or protection of the atua, gods, was withdrawn and it was certain that the transgressor would suffer.

Tapu afforded protection to anything to which it was attached. Thus a fishing ground that was depleted might be preserved through the imposition of a tapu known as a rāhui, which is rather like a trespass law. Projects such as building whare or waka and making kupenga, fishing nets, were similarly protected.

Of course, once the project was completed or a fishing ground was judged to be well stocked again, then it was necessary to remove the tapu and restore a noa state. This process is known as whakanoa. The whakanoa ceremonies were carried out by tohunga, priests or experts, who spent years learning how to navigate the spiritual world.

Through their constant interaction with the laws of tapu the tohunga assumed a very tapu state themselves – so much so that they had to be given their food by way of a stalk or feeding funnel to ensure that there was no physical contact with the head, the most tapu part of the body.

The Māori view of the spiritual world is very refined. It is not a question of life after death being spent in heaven or hell. There are many heavens with different levels of elevation along with a number of other worlds that are inhabited by supernatural beings.

There are different sorts of gods, with the supreme god or deity being Io, who is known and prayed to only by the tohunga.

As well as Ranginui and Papatūānuku, the sky father and earth mother, and their children, seven of whom controlled the forces of nature, there are many personifications which help explain the natural world. For example, Hinemoana is the personification of the ocean, and she is in constant battle with Papatūānuku, always eating away at Papa and changing the coastline through the use of her wave offspring. Bays and inlets are known as Te Ngaunga a Hinemoana, the gnawing of Hinemoana.

Te Rēinga.

If you attend a tangi, you will hear the speakers addressing the tūpāpaku, corpse, and wishing it a speedy journey to the final resting place, Hawaiki, the place where the Māori originated. In Aotearoa there is a set path that the wairua, the spirit of the recently departed, takes through the country to finally arrive at Te Rēinga, the sacred departure place for Hawaiki. This is at Cape Rēinga, which is at the northern tip of Te Ika a Māui, the North Island.

MĀUI

Now that you know how the world was created we'll look at how this land, Aotearoa, came to be. This story involves one of the many surreal episodes in the life of Māui, a superhero – half-man, half-supernatural being.

Māui performed many deeds which ensured lasting benefits for the people among whom he chose to spend his time on earth.

Māui's mother, Taranga, abandoned him at birth, thinking he was stillborn. She wrapped Māui in the topknot of her hair and placed him in the ocean. It was one evening when Taranga and her four sons Māui-taha, Māui-roto, Māui-pae, and Māui-waho were gathered in their whare, that Māui chose to make his reappearance with his family. The family was initially filled with disbelief, but Māui convinced them with his knowledge of the family and Taranga eventually embraced her youngest son and, in recognition of his earlier abandonment, bestowed the name by which Māui has ever since been known: Māui-tikitiki-a-Taranga, Māui of the topknot of Taranga.

Having rejoined his human family, Māui set about performing feats to improve their world. His feats were not always philanthropic in nature though, as he was a natural trickster who enjoyed fooling his fellow men; for example, his sister's husband so annoyed Māui that he turned him into a dog.

However, let's turn to the deeds of Māui that bestowed lasting benefits on the people.

With the help of his brothers, Māui slowed the passage of the sun through the sky so that the people were able to enjoy daylight for much longer. He did this by snaring the sun in a net as it rose to make its quick daily journey. This was also how the people were taught to make nets which they could use to increase their catches of fish.

Māui obtained fire for the people by tricking his grandmother into giving it to him.

Luckily for us, Māui proved to be a great fisherman. It was on a fishing trip with his brothers that he displayed his magical powers with his fishing-line that was equipped with a very special hook, made from the jawbone of his grandmother. Māui's brothers had refused to take him fishing as he had a habit of annoying them with his tricks. However, Māui had risen well before his brothers on the day of the fishing trip and had secreted himself in the floor of the waka. He did not reveal his presence to his bros until they had travelled far from shore. The brothers were angry that they had again been tricked by Māui, but got on with their fishing anyway. When Māui asked if he could have a go they replied, 'No line, no fish . . . sorry bro.' However, Māui did have his own line, and duly convinced his brothers to let him use it. When they refused to give him bait for his hook, Māui made himself bleed and smeared some of his blood on the hook, which he then cast into the ocean.

And, wouldn't you know it, Māui hauled up a huge fish which, still today, is known as Te Ika a Māui, the fish of Māui. And this land of Māui's was where our first ancestors landed ashore after their long journey from Eastern Polynesia. It's also known as the North Island of New Zealand. The waka in which Māui caught his fish is Te Waka a Māui, the canoe of Māui – equally well known as the South Island of New Zealand.

And so Māui provided a place for his people to come to when circumstances eventually forced them to leave their homeland.

On an outing with friends one day Māui attempted to defeat death by entering one of his ancestors, the goddess of death, Hinenuitepō. Before making his attempt Māui cautioned his friends, the birds, not to make a sound lest Hinenuitepō should awaken. Well, so funny did the birds find Māui's efforts to enter Hinenuitepō, they could not contain themselves and they burst into twittering laughter which woke Hinenuitepō who, upon discovering Māui, promptly squeezed him to death!

MIGRATION

There are a number of different theories as to the how, why, and when Māori arrived and settled in this land. And there are theories, too, about exactly where they came from.

How did the Māori come to be in Aotearoa? Some say it was as a result of being out fishing and suddenly being swept away by tempestuous seas and winds which finally brought the hapless ones to the beautiful shores of their new homeland.

It's also posited that a large group of Māori had set out to sail to a neighbouring island when the seas and winds decided to intervene and deposited them in a faraway land that is now known as Aotearoa/New Zealand.

Another theory, again in the fishing vein, is that several brothers were out fishing one day when one of them – Māui – hauled up a huge fish complete with rivers, lakes, forests, mountains … yes, you've guessed it, Te Ika a Māui.

A theory which, until the latter part of the twentieth century, enjoyed wide support among Māori and European academics was the migration theory. It has its roots in myths and chants that list the canoes and various crews that took part in the crossing of Te Moana nui a Kiwa, the Pacific Ocean, to settle in and colonise their new land. This theory can be said to support two different claims as to how the Māori came here: the first, which says that the canoes were simply blown off course while undertaking a much shorter trip to neighbouring islands; and the second, which maintains that the Polynesians were master mariners and navigators. The second theory says that the canoes' captains and navigators knew exactly where they were sailing to. They were journeying to Aotearoa, the land previously visited and named by two of their ancestors, Kupe and Ngahue, in about the tenth century. These two famous Polynesian explorers are said to have named Aotea, white cloud (Great Barrier Island), and Aotearoa, long white cloud (the North Island). After making land in the north they sailed on down to the south where they discovered the highly valued pounamu – greenstone or jade – in the waters of that land which they named Waipounamu, greenstone waters (the South Island). Kupe and Ngahue eventually returned home and told their peoples about the beautiful lands they had discovered, and showed them greenstone they had brought back.

And that was that for another two hundred years or so.

Around the twelfth century an intrepid sailor named Whātonga was swept away by a gale as he took part in an ocean canoe race. He eventually beached in the Bay of Plenty where he was welcomed by the people already living there. Whātonga settled and married in this area and was eventually joined by his grandfather Toi, who had been searching the seas for his lost grandson. Some would say that this was the beginning of the Polynesian colonisation of Aotearoa. Toi and Whātonga's descendants lived happily with the people who had preceded them to the land by some two hundred years, during which time more of their Polynesian people continued to arrive and take up residence.

It was from the existing population, who have become known as the Moriori, and from the new Polynesian arrivals that the Māori people are said to have emerged. As the new people grew in strength and numbers there developed tensions and then wars with the Moriori, who were forced to take refuge in the interior of the Bay of Plenty. Maungapōhatu was one such place of refuge. It is part of the tribal area of the Tūhoe people, who claim to have been part of Aotearoa for much longer than the tribes who trace to the Migration Fleet. This claim is quite understandable in view of Tūhoe's roots among the Moriori. Another place of refuge for the Moriori was Wharekauri, the Chatham Islands, where their descendants were discovered in 1791 when the Vancouver store ship, the *Chatham* called at the islands.

The Moriori are said to be descendants of three canoes, *Taikoria, Kahutara,* and *Okoki*, which were swept away from their homeland by a gale and eventually rode up onto the beach on the north Taranaki coast, where they settled. There is a small settlement called Okoki in north Taranaki today and the Māori from this area are related to the Moriori of Wharekauri. It's quite a trek from north Taranaki to the Bay of Plenty, so there were probably other Moriori canoes like these three.

Now, while there was strife among the emerging new Māori race and the Moriori, so also was there strife and consequent power struggles in the Polynesian homeland. Just where the homeland is or was is another area for debate. Some say it is South America, citing the presence in New Zealand of the kūmara or sweet potato, which is native to South America. Some say it is southern Asia, with India, Malaysia and Taiwan often put forward as the ancient homeland of the Polynesians who came here. It is interesting to note that there are many words in Bahasa Malaysia (the official language of Malaysia) that are exactly the same, and have the same meaning, as words in the Māori/language. And the Malay language is largely derived from the language of the early Middle Eastern traders who settled Malaysia. Of course, many of the languages of the South Pacific are similar to Māori.

To the Māori, however, the homeland is Hawaiki, the location of which has been lost in the mists of time. Tahiti is often suggested as being one and the same as Hawaiki. In Tahiti is Rangiātea, which is a tapu place often referred to in Māori chants. It is also held that there were several Hawaiki and that it was the departure place for the canoes to start their great ocean-crossing journeys. The canoes could well have had different departure places – this makes sense when we realise that the Polynesians were a great seafaring people – who could even fish up countries from the ocean depths!

Wherever Hawaiki is or was, it seems to have experienced serious overcrowding in the late thirteenth and early fourteenth centuries. Food and other resources needed to sustain the population became scarce, and this in turn resulted in tensions and battles for survival among the people. And so some of them decided that the time had come to find a new homeland. But where to go? 'What about that place that Kupe and then Toi and Whātonga described to our ancestors? Aotearoa. Sounds like there's plenty of everything there, even our treasured pounamu. Let's go there.'

Aotearoa One. Te Wānanga o Aotearoa.

And so they did. A fleet of canoes set out for Aotearoa. These canoes that made the crossing of Te Moana nui a Kiwa, were double-hulled canoes connected by a platform with a small cabin on it. The canoes had one or two masts, with a triangular sail. There is debate as to whether the canoes all went together, and also as to the number of canoes that made the migratory journey. However, there are songs that refer to seven well known canoes: *Tainui, Te Arawa, Tokomaru, Tākitimu, Mātaatua, Kurahaupō* and *Aotea*. So let's see what happened to them.

Tainui landed at Kāwhia and the descendants of the crew settled that area and large inland areas now known as Waikato and up to Tāmaki Makaurau (Auckland).

Te Arawa landed initially at Whangapāraoa in the Bay of Plenty and then went on to Maketū, where its people settled and gradually spread inland to Rotorua, with groups going further south to settle around Lake Taupō and the volcanic plateau.

Mātaatua landed near Whakatane in the Bay of Plenty. Whakatāne (to act like a man) got its name from the heroic actions of the daughter of Tōroa the canoe captain. This woman awoke on the shore of the river where the *Mātaatua* was berthed, only to see the canoe beginning to float away on the tide. She was alone and had to exert the strength of a man – whakatāne – to pull the canoe back to shore.

Tokomaru beached at the Mohakatino River in north Taranaki and its people settled from there to around New Plymouth

Tākitimu landed on the East Coast of Te Ika a Māui and its people settled in and around Tūranga, or Gisborne.

Kurahaupō landed in North Auckland where its people settled and later on

'Ohh, someone's beaten us here, bro!'

some of them moved to south Taranaki and an area between Wanganui and Lake Horowhenua.

Aotea landed at the harbour which is now named Aotea Harbour. Turi, the captain of the Aotea, led the people overland through Taranaki and eventually they settled south Taranaki and spread up the Whanganui River.

There were other canoes that made the crossing but the seven mentioned above are the best known ones. Of these the *Te Arawa* was the first to set out on what is now thought to have been a journey that was part of a migratory period, as opposed to being a member of a migration fleet.

So that is how our Māori ancestors came to this land. They were Polynesians but became known as Māori, as a people. The word 'māori ' literally means 'natural' or 'indigenous' and although the word has come to be used to describe any person of Māori descent, Māori really identify themselves by their tribal affiliations – so an indigenous person of Aotearoa New Zealand will think of themselves as Tūhoe or Ngāpuhi or Te Ātiawa or whatever their tribal allegiance happens to be.

WAKA / IWI

Ko Tokomaru te waka, ko Taranaki te maunga, ko Waitara te awa, ko
Paora taku ingoa.

Tokomaru is my canoe, Taranaki is my mountain, Waitara is my river,
and my name is Paul.

This saying defines my tribal affiliation – what canoe my ancestors came on and the sacred mountain and important river in our tribal territory. Pepeha or tribal sayings such as this are often heard in the speeches on the marae at meetings between tribes. When Māori hear a pepeha they recognise the identity of the speaker. The name of the waka immediately narrows the possible origins of the speaker. The names of the mountain and river confirm to listeners that the speaker belongs to one of seven or so tribes of central and northern Taranaki.

The speaker will then often proceed to give his or her parents' names and their tribal affiliations before expounding whatever argument the speaker has risen to speak to. It maybe that the speaker's whakapapa contains links to the iwi, tribe, upon whose land the speaker is standing, in which case that link is often disclosed to the listeners before the speaker launches into the core of his or her kōrero or speech.

Identity is crucial in Māori culture. On meeting a newcomer, Māori will usually attempt to establish that person's identity by first inquiring as to where the newcomer is from. Next will come questions as to whether or not the person knows or is related to various people from their home area known to the questioner. The answers build a picture of the newcomer's tribal identity and help to establish tribal relationships for the questioner.

Iwi are made up of whānau, families, and hapū, extended family groups. All iwi trace to a waka and, through intermarriage, whānau and hapū will inevitably trace to several waka. These connections have been the reasons for iwi and hapū to unite in times of war. They have also provided the basis for wars and battles to be settled by marriages or negotiated settlements when past links have been brought to the fore by one of the warring parties.

Such links also provide the base of evidence for claims to land. Each waka has its own descended iwi and, through these iwi, its own rohe or tribal district.

Waka in action.

NGĀ INGOA WĀHI
PLACENAMES

The land that each tribe occupied – and occupies – is extremely important to them, materially, culturally and emotionally. One way in which a tribe maps out its landscape and treasures it, is by marking it with placenames. In one aspect Māori placenames are no different to those anywhere else in the world. Unless you know the tale of how a particular place came by its name, then you may well know how to read, pronounce and even understand the language of the placename, but you won't really know the meaning of it. And this can lead to misunderstandings. For example, the name Urenui in Taranaki could be understood as 'massive penis' or 'great courage'. In this particular case, understanding might be assisted by the local school motto, 'Upward and Upright'.

Often placenames reflect aspects of the landscape. For example, Waitangi: wai = water, and tangi = singing. Other placenames refer back to an incident in tribal history, such as Whakatāne (see 'Migration'). Māori tribal history can be traced through the origins of placenames and it is a fascinating pastime seeking the correct meanings.

Here are some examples of placenames and their translations.

Waiwera: wai = water, wera = hot. Waiwera is a small tourist resort about forty minutes north of Auckland, on the Hibiscus Coast. Its main attractions are the thermal pools and spa.

Rotorua: roto = lake, rua = two or second. Rotorua is said to be the second lake discovered by one of the ancestors of Te Arawa, Ihenga, who named it in honour of his father-in-law, Kahu. The full name is Roto-rua-nui-a-Kahu.

Kaikōura: kai = food/to eat, kōura = crayfish. Kaikōura is located on the northern east coast of the South Island, Te Waka a Māui, and it is famous for the amount of crayfish caught in its waters. It's also famous as the place to go whale-watching, but that's another tale.

Kaikōura is famous for its kōura.

There are some placenames which you can understand only if you know what took place there.

Rangitoto: rangi = sky or day, toto = blood. Rangitoto is an island in the Hauraki Gulf to the east of Auckland. It was the scene of a disagreement between Tamatekapua and Hoturoa, two captains of the migration canoes. Tamatekapua had been paying far too much attention to Hoturoa's wife and Hoturoa tackled him about his behaviour. In the ensuing exchange Tamatekapua was wounded and his blood flowed. So the island was named to mark this incident. The full name is Te RangitotongiaaTamatekapua, the day that Tamatekapua's blood flowed.

Some placenames have been given in memory of the original homeland, Hawaiki.

Rangiātea: rangi = sky, ātea = space. Rangiātea occurs at several locations around Aotearoa, with perhaps the best known being the church at Ōtaki which was named Rangiātea by Te Rauparaha. Rangiātea is the Māori version of Ra'iatea, a sacred place in Hawaiki.

Motutapu: motu = island, tapu = sacred. This name occurs in several places around Aotearoa. Again, it is a name brought from Hawaiki.

Hikurangi: hiku = point or summit, rangi = sky. There are several places so-named in Aotearoa, including Mt Hikurangi, which is on the east coast of the North

Island where, as well as being the sacred mountain of the Ngāti Porou iwi, it is the first place to see the sun each day. This is another name from Hawaiki.

There are also other ingoa wāhi, or placenames, where European placenames have simply been translated into Māori. On the Whanganui River are several places whose names are the Māori transliterations of overseas city names.

Hiruharama is Māori for Jerusalem – and was named by an early missionary, Rev. Richard Taylor. It became well known in the late 1960s as the location for the followers of Kiwi poet James K. Baxter. Other settlements along the river are Rānana (London), Ātene (Athens) and Koroniti (Corinth).

And there are a number of placenames which are simply what the European scribes mistakenly thought was the correct name – for example, Ōtākau has become known as Otago.

Bearing in mind that the listed placename may not necessarily be the full name and may therefore not disclose the story behind the name, it is often possible to discern the meaning by looking at the component parts of the name. This is particularly so in respect of names that reflect their surrounding environments.

And so to assist you in your placename-meaning quest, here's a list of Māori words which are common component parts of Māori placenames, along with their translations.

awa = river, channel, gully or valley	manga = stream
wai = water	te = the
ngā = the (plural)	kaha = strong, energetic
moana = sea, ocean	nui = large, plenty, many
iti = small, few	kai = food, eat
roa = long	whaka = to make like, assume form of
manu = bird	rangi = sky, weather, day
whanga = bay, inlet, stretch of water	hoki = return

Koroniti marae.

rua = two, hole, potato	tahi = one
whare = house	motu = nation, island
ahi = fire	ao = cloud, world
atua = god, deity	maunga = mountain
mutu = end, finish	one = beach, sand, soil
pā = fortified village	pae = ridge, range of hills
pō = night	puke = hill
aka = vine	roto = lake
whenua = land, country, placenta	pai = good
puna = spring of water	hua = fruit
ika = fish	tai = sea, tide, coast, wave

And that brings me to the longest placename in Aotearoa and, according to some, in the world:

Taumatawhakatangihangakōauauotamateaturipūkakapikimaungahoronuku pōkaiwhenuakitanatahu

The place where Tamatea, the man with big knees, who slid, climbed, and was well travelled, played the flute to his loved one …
(source www.hawkesbaynz.com).

You can visit this place in Hawke's Bay.

Longest placename. *Hawke's Bay Inc.*

NGĀ KŌRERO TUKU IHO
MĀORI ORAL TRADITION

Before the arrival of the missionaries there was no written Māori language. Tribal history, genealogies, legends and myths were passed on through various vehicles which make up the great Māori oral tradition. These vehicles — formal speeches, (whaikōrero), songs (waiata), proverbial sayings (whakataukī), tribal sayings (pepeha), and karakia (incantations) — still exist and are employed today on the marae.

Formal whaikōrero, speeches, on the marae follow a pattern which includes acknowledgement and greetings to the marae, the wharenui (the meeting house), te hunga mate (those who have passed on; the dead), te hunga ora (the living), and to the manuhiri (visitors). Within these speeches will be references to ancestors of both the speaker and the manuhiri, Hawaiki, the path that the spirits must follow in order to reach their final resting place, and to whakapapa (genealogical connections) between the tangata whenua (hosts), and the manuhiri. The art of whaikōrero is largely learned through listening to accomplished exponents of that artform on the marae.

There are karakia for all occasions in the Māori world. These karakia must be learned by the people selected as worthy to carry the sacred knowledge contained within the karakia. These karakia are often not written down; they are passed on by oral means and are committed to memory by students.

All races have their store of sayings that people use to colour their written and spoken language. Māori have a big store of them, because sayings and proverbs were a great way of remembering things in an oral tradition. Many have been handed down through generations. Some will disappear as they become less relevant, while some will no doubt still be being used by orators and people in the next millennium. Many can be recognised as having similar meanings to sayings in other languages. Following are some Māori sayings, and the equivalent English proverb where appropriate.

He manako te kōura i kōre ai.
Crayfish are scarce when they are expected.
(Don't count your chickens before they hatch.)

Mā whero mā pango ka oti te mahi.
By red and black a job is finished.
(Many hands make light work.)

Ngaro atu he tētēkura, whakaeke mai he tētēkura.
When one chief disappears, another is ready.
(No one is indispensable.)

Some sayings derive from an incident in tribal history and so are important markers of traditions but they can also come to have a generalised meaning, such as:

He kura pae nā Mahina.
It is a treasure found by Mahina washed up on the shore.

This is truly an oldie, but a goodie. There are variations on whether Mahina was the person who lost or who found the kura – as you might expect after 1000 years or so. Let's assume he was the person who found the kura. Legend has it that some of the people on the migratory canoes were overcome by the sight of the red flowering pōhutukawa trees that lined the shore where the canoes made landfall in Aotearoa. The pōhutukawa flower looked just like the kura, red features, held on the canoes. The kura was a treasure brought from the explorers' homeland. However, with kura growing on trees, why hold onto the ones that had travelled so far and had no

Pōhutukawa on the coast. *Robert Key*

doubt become a little worn? So the kura were thrown overboard and subsequently washed up on the shore, where Mahina found one and later refused to return it to the original owner.

And so we have . . . Finders keepers. And we also have 'Losers weepers' when the travellers discovered that their instant kura soon faded and died.

Ahakoa he iti kete, he iti nā te aroha.
Although it is a small basket, it is given with love.
(It is the thought that counts.)

E koa koe ināianei, ā, māku hoki te rā āpōpō.
You're happy now, but tomorrow will be my turn.
(He who laughs last, laughs loudest.)

He ora te whakapiri, he mate te whakatākiri.
(United we stand, divided we fall.)

He harore rangi tahi.
A mushroom lasts a day.
(Here today, gone tomorrow.)

He pai rangi tahi.
The joy of a single day.
(Short and sweet.)

Moea te tāne me te ringa raupā.
Marry the man with blistered hands – a worker.

An important way of passing on knowledge is the use of waiata, songs which, in the Māori world, have many forms. A waiata may reveal aspects of a tribe's history, or it may tell of a current or past love of the composer. Other waiata outline the tribal area boundaries and features within those boundaries. The names of the seven best known canoes of the migration period are recorded in the waiata 'Ngā Waka e Whitu' (the seven canoes). Aspects of genealogy are present in many waiata and it is through these that iwi become familiar with their tribal heritage and history.

There are a great variety of types of waiata within Maoridom. In addition to songs of love, waiata aroha, there are songs of lament, waiata tangi, and songs which use the poi (ball on a string) to emphasise the message of the lyric, waiata poi. Songs composed for and dedicated to the composer's lover, waiata whaiāipo. Songs that are composed in reply to other songs, which may have cast aspersions on the people of the composer, who is moved to compose a reply, are waiata whakautu.

There are the waiata of welcome, which are called out by women to manuhiri, visitors, as they enter onto the host marae. Such waiata are called karanga. There are special waiata that the host workers will sometimes sing as they serve food to their guests. These are called waiata hari kai

Many of the different types of waiata are performed with accompanying actions and these are known generically as action songs or waiata-ā-ringa. In the early to middle twentieth century, many waiata a ringa were set to existing European song melodies. The messages and lyrics of these waiata have nothing in common with those of the European lyrics. It is the melody that is the important aspect of the composer's cultural adaption. The composer has chosen it because it is widely known and liked by Māori and, as such, it will make a suitable vehicle to gain widespread and quick acceptance of their waiata.

Haka.

There are other songs, called pao, which are similar to a 'ditty', and these address topical issues. Of course there are lullabies, oriori; and there is a type of waiata that is composed by women who have been slandered – these are called pātere. A type of waiata that is usually the domain of the men is the haka and, as you will see in a later chapter, there are a variety of these.

One of the best known of all waiata is 'Pōkarekare ana' – a waiata aroha. You will hear this anywhere in the world where Kiwis are gathered and feeling a bit homesick. Here are the words and translation of 'Pōkarekare ana'. Depending on where the singers are from, the name of the waters being crossed by the composer's lover may vary.

Pōkarekare Ana

As arranged by P.H. Tomoana and his Concert Party, 1917

1

Pōkarekare ana
ngā wai o Waiapu
whiti atu koe hine
marino ana e.

May the rough waters
of Waiapu
that you are crossing
become calm.

(chorus)

E hine e
hoki mai rā
ka mate ahau
i te aroha e.

Oh my dear
please return to me
or I shall die
without your love.

2

Tuhituhi taku reta
tuku atu taku ringi
kia kito tō iwi
raruraru ana e.

(chorus)

I have written my letter
I have posted you my ring
so you can show your people
who are disbelieving.

3

E kore te aroha
e maroke e te rā.
Mākūkū tonu
i aku roimata e.
(chorus)

My love will not
be dried up by the sun.
It will be nurtured
by my tears.

4

Whatiwhati taku pene
kua pau aku pepa
ko taku aroha
mau tonu ana e.
(chorus ends song)

My pen is broken
and I've run out of paper
but my love for you
still remains.

Waiata poi.

TE REO
THE MĀORI LANGUAGE

The Māori language originated in Polynesia and, not surprisingly, there are similarities between all of the Polynesian languages of the Pacific. The closest of these languages to that of Māori is that of the Cook Islands, which is held by many to be the last casting-off place during the migration period. Similarities, though, are just what the word implies and each country has developed its own language. And within those countries there also exist a number of sub-languages, dialects that are spoken within tribal boundaries. New Zealand is no different in this regard, although there tends to be a certain amount of homogeneity in the oral language, particularly since the 1970s when te reo began to be widely taught within institutions as opposed to being passed down via the marae or home.

The Māori alphabet consists of fifteen letters, two of which are diagraphs, 'ng' and 'wh'. There are five vowels and eight consonants. The vowels are listed below, along with English words to assist you with correct pronunciation. Sometimes the vowel is doubled in length and this is indicated by the placing of a macron over the vowel.

Vowel	short, as in	long, as in
a	along	tar
o	fed	beg
i	key	sheep
o	or	awe
u	foot	toot

Digraph

ng   as in song

wh   usually an 'f' sound, e.g. funk, but can also be a 'w' sound as in wall.

Tangata whenua welcome the manuhiri.

Here are some phrases you will find helpful when interacting with Māori speakers. They are listed along with a guide to pronunciation.

Greetings

Hello	Kia ora	key aura
Good morning	Mōrena	more-reh-nah
	Ata mārie	art-a mah-ree-eh
Good afternoon	Ahiahi mārie	ah-he-ah-he ma-ree-eh
Good evening, goodnight	Pō mārie	poor mah-ree-eh
Greetings	Tēnā koe	ten-ah kway (addressing one person)
	Tēnā kōrua	ten-ah cor-roo-ah (addressing two people)
	Tēnā koutou	ten-ah coe-toe (more than two people)
	Tēnā koutou katoa	ten-ah coe-toe car-toh-ah (big crowd)

Farewells

This is what the person departing says:

Goodbye	E noho rā	eh-nor-who-rah

This is what the person staying says:

Goodbye	Haere rā	high-e-reh rah

Small talk

How are you today?	Kei te pēhea koe i tēnei rā?
	kay te pear-here
	kway ee ten-ay rah?
I am fine thank you.	Kei te pai au.
	kay te pie oh.

You can buy a great little Māori/English phrasebook called *Instant! Māori* from most book retailers in New Zealand. Unlike most other such phrasebooks *Instant! Māori* uses phonetics to assist you with pronunciation.

Of course the only reason we are able to write the Māori language is because the Europeans brought the written language to Aotearoa New Zealand. They also brought their own language, which was quickly learned by Māori during the early European contact period as they realised that English was one of the keys to developing trade and relationships with the newcomers. As time went by and the colonisation process gathered pace, numbers of both Māori and Pākehā believed that the future welfare of Māori lay in their adopting the 'European way' and embracing the English language.

The use of te reo Māori declined steadily during the twentieth century. This was assisted by a school policy of physical punishment being meted out to any child caught speaking Māori at school! The decline accelerated during the latter half of the century as more and more Māori moved from their traditional rural home areas to the cities. There was, however, a renaissance of things Māori that really took hold in the 1970s, and from that period and into the new millennium there has been a remarkable resurgence of te reo, along with Māori culture generally.

One of the highly influential factors of the resurgence has been the establishment of the national network of kōhanga reo – 'language nests'. These early childhood centres school the kids in te reo. The kids go home at night and speak in te reo to their parents. For many of the parents, te reo is something they have heard on the marae but not spoken. Their children speaking Māori prompts the parents to decide that they had better learn to speak te reo too – can't have the kids showing them up!

The Treaty of Waitangi Act was passed into law in 1975 and, from that time, the resurgence of te reo and things Māori generally has been spectacular.

A rural kōhanga reo.

Māori Language Day was established in 1975 and has since grown to a week, which is widely promoted nationally.

There are Māori owned and operated tertiary institutions, one of which, Te Wānanga o Aotearoa, has the largest number of students of all New Zealand tertiary institutions.

There is a network of Māori owned and operated radio stations, and Te Whakaata Māori, the Māori Television channel, was opened in 2004.

Te reo Māori, the Māori language, now enjoys the status of an official language of New Zealand, and many government department notices such as health and employment advertisements are published in both English and Māori. Television and radio broadcasters have adopted Māori forms of greeting and farewell to address their audiences.

Māori Television presenter. *Te Whakaata Māori/Māori Television*

These gains have their origins in the Treaty of Waitangi, which guarantees that Māori shall enjoy and retain their taonga, treasured possessions, including te reo.

PĀKEHĀ AND THE TREATY OF WAITANGI

The Waitangi Sheet, *ANZ IA 9/9*

Abel Tasman, a Dutch navigator and explorer, is credited as the first European to discover Aotearoa, and it was he who named it New Zealand when he arrived here in 1642. It was over a hundred years later, in 1769, that the first Englishman, Captain James Cook, arrived off the east coast of New Zealand on his ship the *Endeavour*. There are claims of other sea-going explorers having visited Aotearoa before both Tasman and Cook. Some of the iwi of the east coast of the North Island believe that their ancestors were visited by Spanish explorers and that there was intermarriage between the races. They point to the presence of many light-skinned people with light-coloured hair among the iwi today as proof of this.

The early 1800s saw traders, whalers, sealers, convicts, and all sorts of people from many countries settling in New Zealand among the tribes and plying their trades. The traders introduced the musket to the northern Māori tribes at the turn of the century and those iwi proceeded to wreak havoc among the musketless tribes to the south. It was wild. And there was no law enforcement between Māori and Pākehā because there was no authority that held sway over the non-Māori population. These conditions were not ideal for the encouragement of settlers from England.

Missionaries from England began to arrive in Aotearoa in the early 1800s. Their teachings of Christianity were not readily accepted by Māori until the mid 1800s – the missionaries felt that this was in large part due to the lawlessness that existed at the time. The missionaries became a powerful lobby group for the English Crown to establish law and order in New Zealand. There were regular dispatches to church authorities in England bemoaning the behaviour of the non-Māori inhabitants of New Zealand.

The colonisation process which brought the initial settlers from Great Britain to Aotearoa was carried out not by a branch of the English government but by a private company, established by entrepreneur Edward Gibbon Wakefield. The New Zealand Company Ltd was the vehicle that Wakefield used to market New Zealand to prospective settlers in their home countries. When the settlers arrived in the new country they had merely to proceed to their already purchased plot of paradise and get on with the job of establishing a home for themselves and their families. It was not uncommon, however, for disputes to arise over ownership of lands sold under this system. Once the Treaty of Waitangi had been signed all rights of acquiring and purchase of lands held by Māori were assigned to the Crown and its representatives. However, none of this could happen until some sort of agreement regarding law and order and sovereignty had been worked out between the Māori rulers of Aotearoa and the Queen of England, who would be the sovereign for the New Zealand Company settlers.

The English colonial agents were apprehensive of the possibility of French settlers for they had reason to believe that these people intended for New Zealand to become a colonial possession of France. And so a plea was directed to Queen Victoria asking her to enter into a treaty with the chiefs of Maoriland. (For quite some years in the nineteenth and early twentieth century, Aotearoa New Zealand was widely known among the colonial settlers as 'Maoriland'.) The queen agreed to the request and William Hobson, a captain in the Royal Navy, was appointed as her representative with authority to negotiate such a treaty.

Māori were concerned at the number of European people moving into their country. Of course there were advantages, such as those Europeans who became Pākehā Māori and, having taken a Māori wife, proceeded to help the iwi in matters of trade. However, the lawlessness that accompanied the uncontrolled growth was a worry. And so, in this respect, Māori were ready to enter into some sort of agreement with some power that would bring law and order to the non-Māori population. However, they were not ready to give up their own authority over their people, lands or fisheries.

How then was the queen's representative to achieve the signing of a treaty with Māori? Hobson, with the help of James Busby, who was the British Resident, a consular representative in New Zealand since 1833, drafted a treaty. On 4 February 1840, Henry Williams, an influential Anglican missionary, and his son Edward were given one night to translate Hobson and Busby's draft into Māori.

Well, without judging the motives of the Treaty process, here's what happened at the Treaty signing at Waitangi on 6 May 1840. There were two versions of the Treaty – one in Māori and one in English. Nothing unexpected in that. However, when you examine these two treaties, you can clearly see that what the Māori chiefs agreed to was quite different to what the queen's representative *thought* they had agreed to. The Williams, in their translation of the English version into Māori, seem to have added terms which maybe they felt would ensure agreement among Māori.

The key words that have given rise to acrimony between the parties ever since the signing are 'sovereignty', which is translated as 'kāwanatanga', and 'rangatiratanga', which is included in the Māori version but there is no translation of this word in the English version. In addition, the Māori version has a spiritual element in the wording that guarantees Māori possession of all their 'taonga', which translates to treasured possessions and/or spiritual treasures. Taonga can be anything that is held in great respect and is, in fact, treasured. In the late twentieth century the full meaning of the word was still being defined, and newly emergent taonga included the airwaves.

The Treaty became all things to all people. Māori were guaranteed all the rights of English citizens, including the protection of the queen and her forces, and, at the same time, retained full authority, 'rangatiratanga', over their peoples and possessions. The English version guarantees to the Chiefs and Tribes of New Zealand and to the respective families and individuals thereof the full exclusive and undisturbed possession of their Lands and Estates Forests Fisheries and other properties which they may collectively or individually possess so long as it is their wish and desire to retain the same in their possession . . . (Article the Second, The Treaty of Waitangi). But, unlike the Māori version, it does not guarantee the chiefs their continued authority over their people and their lands, possessions, treasures and fisheries.

With the benefit of hindsight one can see that the treaties were a recipe for misunderstanding. However, from a somewhat more cynical point of view, they did buy the colonial agents time – and they proceeded to put that acquisition to immediate use. The immigrant ships came over the oceans to New Zealand and schemes were quickly introduced to acquire as much of the Māori lands as possible in as little time as possible. One of the terms of the Treaty was that Māori were required to deal solely with the Crown in respect of all land sales – which, of course, enabled the Crown and its agents to control land prices.

Throughout the rest of the nineteenth and continuing into the twentieth century Māori complained bitterly at perceived Treaty breaches by the Crown. An early way of the Crown dealing with these complaints was to have the courts declare the treaty a 'nullity'; this was decreed by Chief Justice James Prendergast in 1877.

It was not until one of New Zealand's most charismatic leaders, Norman Kirk, came to power as prime minister in 1972 that things started to change in the way successive governments treated the complaints of their Treaty partners. The Treaty of Waitangi Act 1975 established the Waitangi Tribunal, whose mission was to investigate claims by Māori against the Crown. The Crown, while not recognising the treaty as a legally enforceable document, did take cognisance of the terms of the Act. This period was the beginning of a movement that has seen the establishment of Māori tertiary institutions, media outlets, schools and childcare centres, and the official promotion of the Māori language, which was made an official language of New Zealand under The Māori Language Act 1987.

This is not to say that all's well between the Treaty partners, but it is proof that there is now some goodwill on both sides. And that is the essential element in the achievement of lasting harmony.

The Treaty of Waitangi in both its English and Māori forms can be viewed on the website www.treatyofwaitangi.govt.nz.

TE KĪNGITANGA
MĀORI ROYALTY

To many non-Māori New Zealanders, the Māori queen was the royal head of Maoridom, or the Māori nation. Although this was not actually the case, the asumption is very close to the aspirations of those nineteenth-century Māori rangatira, chiefly leaders, who established the movement that, in due course, anointed its first supreme leader as king in June 1858 at Ngāruawāhia.

Why did they choose the title of king when there had not previously existed such a role in the Māori world?

Well, in 1852 Tāmihana Te Rauparaha, son of Te Rauparaha the famous Ngāti Toa chief (and composer of the world-famous haka 'Ka mate, ka mate'), was presented to Queen Victoria in England. Tāmihana was very impressed by the queen and by the obvious respect and honour which were accorded to her by her subjects. Not to mention HRH's personal power, which extended right around the world, even to this country. Just six years earlier Tāmihana had seen his father, who had lived the life of a warrior and conquered many lands in Aotearoa, seized by the queen's New Zealand representative and held captive for two years. Such an illustration of power! And so, on his return from England, Tāmihana told his father (now free again) that he knew the means whereby the Māori people could gain relief and security from the troubles that were being visited upon them as a result of the European settlers' insatiable demands for land. What the Māori people needed was a supreme protector who would unite the tribes and protect their lands against the settlers' demands. It was obvious to Tāmihana that the most effective such supreme protector was a king, and that king should be his father, Te Rauparaha.

Te Rauparaha could see merit in his son's argument but did not want to accept the office himself. He reminded his son that the reason he and his Ngāti Toa people had left their ancestral home of Kāwhia was because they could not match the power of the Waikato tribes. A king must command great power and his people and lands must be capable of hosting all participating tribes for the inevitable gatherings. His mana, authority, must also be such that his settlement of intertribal disputes would be accepted by parties involved. Such disputes became more common as tribal authority broke down in the face of the continued advances of European and Colonial influences on the Māori world.

Convinced that he held the key to Māori salvation, Tāmihana, aided by his cousin Mātene Te Whiwhi, set off around the North Island canvassing support for the concept of a Māori king and seeking candidates for the position. Over the course of the next six years, the position of king was offered to many of the reigning chiefs in the North Island. After each rejection of the offer, the path to the kingship seemed to lead more and more towards Waikato. Their leaders had in 1854 laid a tapu that outlawed the sale of lands within their boundaries.

It was a reluctant Pōtatau Te Wherowhero, rangatira or high chief of the Waikato iwi Ngāti Mahuta, who accepted the mantle of king in June 1858 at Ngāruawāhia. Although Pōtatau's health was not good, he was an ideal candidate and his appointment established the royal lines of descent for his successors. Pōtatau was a consummate warrior, whose fighting skills were such that he was known far and wide by the saying, 'Ko Te Wherowhero, te ana o te tangata' (It is Te Wherowhero, the cavern of men). This saying or pepeha pays tribute to Pōtatau by making him the cavern into which so many men had disappeared, never to be seen again. At his coronation Pōtatau made the following proclamation:

Kōtahi anō te kōhao o te ngira e kuhuna ai te mira mā, te mira pango, te mira whero.

There is only one eye of the needle through which must pass the white thread, the black thread, and the red thread.

These do not sound like the words of someone setting up a separatist movement that wants nothing whatsoever to do with the non-Māori occupants of the land.

And yet, from its inception, the Māori King Movement, the Kīngitanga, was regarded with deep suspicion by settlers and colonial governments alike. It came to be regarded as a 'land league' which, to the colonial government, was a serious affront to their aims of wresting as much land from the Māori as possible.

The king's original areas of influence and adherence included Hauraki, Waikato-Maniapoto, Kāwhia, Taupō, Mōkau, parts of Taranaki, the upper Whanganui, upper Rangitikei and Titiokura. The main tribal groups that resisted inclusion under the king's mana were the Northland tribes, most of Te Arawa, most of Ngāti Porou and the other East Coast tribes, and most of the South Island. But even in these latter areas there were strong pockets of support for the Kīngitanga.

The scene was set for confrontation.

On the one side a movement that forbade any land sales unless sanctioned by the king and, on the other, colonial forces and settlers who had come to start a new life in this land of plenty . . . of land.

Pōtatau died in 1860 and was succeeded by his son Tāwhiao, who went on to reign for thirty-four years. Government forces invaded the Waikato in 1863, and in 1864 the Kīngitanga forces withdrew into the lands south of Te Awamutu and Kihikihi. They remained the governing force in this area, which became known as the King Country, for nearly twenty years. However, the punishment for resisting the invasion of their ancestral lands was that the Waikato peoples lost 1.2 million acres to confiscation by the Crown.

Tāwhiao formally laid down his arms to the colonial government in 1881 at Alexandra, near Pirongia. On that occasion he declared, 'This is the end of warfare in this land.' Tāwhiao had adopted the Pai Mārire faith and refined it to his own version, which is called 'Tariao'. This is a pacifist-based religion and it may well be that, in adopting it, he recognised that no amount of fighting could redress the past wrongs wrought on his people.

It was time for a change. So Tāwhiao concentrated on building loyalty to the Kīngitanga. He instituted the Poukai, whereby the king paid annual visits to loyal marae and listened to what his supporters had to say. In 1884 he led a deputation to England with a petition for Queen Victoria, 'To have the Treaty honoured'.

The King Movement established its own newspapers, the first of which, *Te Hokioi e Rere atu na*, was published in the late 1850s. *Te Hokioi* ceased publication in 1863 and its presses are now at the Te Awamutu Museum. It was followed by *Te Paki o Matariki*.

Tāwhiao established his own parliament, Te Kauhanganui, in the late 1880s at Maungakawa. In 1886 he established Te Peeke o Aotearoa (The Bank of New Zealand), which operated until 1905.

Tāwhiao died in August 1894 and was succeeded by his son Mahuta. Soon after Mahuta's succession, Te Kauhanganui announced the setting up of 'the Kingdom's own courts for land, civil and criminal cases'. Judges, registrars, police and clerks were appointed. Taxes were imposed. A minister of lands was appointed. Spokesmen to mediate tribal disputes were also appointed, and King Movement schools were planned. Many of these plans foundered, however, through Crown resistance and a simple lack of resources.

In 1903 Mahuta accepted an offer from Premier Seddon of a seat on the legislative council, and he was sworn in as a member of the executive council. He did not enjoy his time on either council and, as a result of his accepting Seddon's offer, a split developed within the King Movement. There was another movement that was proceeding parallel with Te Kīngitanga, called Te Kotahitanga. The aims of this movement were to unite Māori and to establish their own parliament, which would govern them. Of course Mahuta already had his parliament, but he did see the merit in unity and made some unsuccessful attempts to unite Kīngitanga and Kotāhitanga. Upon Mahuta's appointment to the executive and legislative councils, the Kīngitanga began to lose support to the Kotahitanga.

In 1907 TT Rawhiti, King Mahuta's private secretary, played a prominent part in the promotion of Te Kotahitanga, which included a petition to King Edward VII to treat Māori and European equally in terms of the Treaty of Waitangi.

These were trying times for the Kīngitanga – and they were soon to get tougher. Mahuta died and was succeeded by his son Te Rata in 1912. The First World

War brought fresh problems for the Kīngitanga. In 1881 Tāwhiao had declared that he would no longer support war. Partly as a result of Tāwhiao's words and partly because none of Waikato's grievances had been addressed, Kīngitanga supporters were advised that no one should volunteer for the war. This resulted in many young men, including members of the royal family, being arrested and placed in military training camps. The government used conscription to call up men for the war effort, but among Māori this was only used on Waikato and Maniapoto peoples.

In May 1914 Te Rata and his advisors went to England and presented another petition to King George and Queen Mary. Although they were apparently politely received there was nothing forthcoming from the Crown. What we are seeing here is confirmation of the views held by Māori from the time of the Treaty signing that their agreement under that document was with the queen – not the colonial governments, who kept coming between them and the queen. These trips to England to seek redress for wrongs thrust upon them through breaches of the Treaty were a feature of Māori political life throughout the latter half of the nineteenth century and the early twentieth century. It's quite likely that they would continue even now (to the Privy Council, though, as opposed to the Queen) had the government not removed the right of access of its citizens to the Privy Council in the late twentieth century.

In 1920 Waikato leaders were able to buy 10 acres of confiscated land on the bank of the Waikato River opposite Ngāruawāhia. One wonders if the sellers realised that by this sale they made possible the prophetic proclamation of the long departed Tāwhiao: 'Ko Arekahanara taku hāona kaha, ko Kemureti taku oko horoi, ko Ngāruawāhia taku tūrangawaewae' ('Alexandra [Pirongia] is my horn of strength, Cambridge is my washbowl, and Ngāruawāhia is my footstool (literally my place to stand, or my home'). It was King Tāwhiao's grandaughter Te Puea who led the movement to establish Ngāruawāhia as the site of the Kīngitanga's tūrangawaewae, thereby realising her grandfather's prophecy.

In 1919 Taingākawa, adviser to Tāwhiao and Te Rata, asked Prime Minister William Massey to have the Treaty placed on record as an imperial document. He should have known that that was the last thing any colonial government wanted to do with the Treaty!

Tūrangawaewae.

In 1923 Taingākawa presented a petition to the government for a commission of inquiry into the land confiscations of the 1860s. The petition was based on the rights accorded Māori under the Treaty.

In 1924 Taingākawa joined T.W. Ratana's trip to London to present another petition and to seek the intervention of the League of Nations.

Te Rata did not enjoy good health and, during the 1920s, he withdrew his mouthpiece role from his Kauhanganui and more and more came to rely on Te Puea, whose father was Te Tahuna Hērangi, the son of an English surveyor, William Searancke.Te Puea's mother was Hāriata Rangitaupa of the Ngāti Maniapoto hapū Ngāti Ngāwaero.

Te Puea devoted herself to the welfare of the many children who were orphaned as a result of the influenza epidemic of 1918. Partly because of this and partly through her desire to realise her grandfather's prophecy concerning Ngāruawāhia as his tūrangawaewae, Te Puea assumed the responsibility of establishing and building the future home of the King Movement on the 10 acres purchased by Waikato leaders in 1920.

Waikato people stayed away from the 1940 Treaty Centennial celebrations which they viewed as an occasion for rejoicing on the part of the Pākehā and the Māori whose tribes had not suffered any injustices during the preceding hundred years.

However, some progress was being made towards addressing the grievances of Waikato and, in 1946, Te Puea accepted an offer from Prime Minister Peter Fraser of an annual payment of five thousand pounds to the Tainui Trust Board. This offer was not accepted by Waikato as settlement of their grievances but rather as an acknowledgement by the Crown that there were legitimate grievances that needed to be addressed. As indeed they would be, in due course.

Te Puea devoted her life to the Kīngitanga. She was able to increase its standing among Europeans by inviting leaders of the day to Tūrangawaewae. When Te Puea died in 1952, both the prime minister and the opposition leader of the day attended her tangi, and the BBC devoted a broadcast to her memory.

Te Rata died in 1933 and was succeeded by his son Korokī, who guided the Kīngitanga until his death in 1966 when he in turn was succeeded by his daughter, Te Atairangikahu, who upon her coronation assumed the title of Te Arikinui Te Atairangikahu. The first Māori queen was also known as Dame Te Atairangikahu, Dame Te Ata and, to her own people, The Lady.

Dame Te Ata was devoted to the improvement of the welfare of the Māori people and to the retention and spreading of the Māori culture. In 1979 she led a delegation to the government of the day seeking the establishment of an organisation whose role would be to foster the growth of te reo Māori, the Māori language. That meeting led to the establishment of kōhanga reo (see 'Te Reo'), a network of childcare centres that use te reo Māori as their medium of communication and teaching. Dame Te Ata was the patron of kōhanga reo, and she was also the patron of one of the most influential Māori organisations, the Maori Women's Welfare League.

One of the most significant events that Te Atairangikahu oversaw in her time at the helm was the settlement of the grievances that all her predecessors had sought to have the Crown address since the inception of the Kīngitanga. On 3 November 1995 Queen Elizabeth II signed into law the Waikato Tainui Raupatu Claims Settlement Bill in the presence of Te Arikinui Te Atairangikahu, Tainui's principal negotiator, Robert Te Kotahi Mahuta, and other Tainui elders. This was the first iwi settlement for crown breaches of the Treaty of Waitangi.

Justice at last!

On 15 August 2006, Dame Te Atairangikahu passed away, and Aotearoa as a nation was united in mourning her passing. She had touched the lives of so many people, Māori and Pākehā during her reign. For seven days and nights the national media was devoted to the tangi, funeral, of the first Māori queen. It was truly a historic occasion. Through the foresight of the Tainui authorities in allowing the national

Te Atairangikahu's casket being carried from the waka to Taupiri Mountain.

media total access to the tangi and burial, the nation was able to participate in and observe the tangihanga and the moving farewells accorded to Te Atairangikahu by Māori and Pākehā. Farewells from other races and nations continued to flow into Ngāruawāhia from around the world, bringing to mind the words of the first Māori king Te Whero whero: 'Kotahi anō te kōhao o te ngira e kuhuna ai te mira pango, te mira ma, te mira whero.'

Mourners at Taupiri Mountain.

The position of king or queen, leader of the Kīngitanga, is an elected one, not hereditary. The leaders of the tribes that support the Kīngitanga are the people that decide who shall succeed to the position left vacant by the passing of an incumbent. The Tainui leaders do not take part in the election process, which could result in the position of king or queen moving outside of Tainui to another tribal group. The position of monarch has, however, remained within Tainui since the inception of the Kīngitanga. There has also been maintained an unbroken family line of succession that was established with the appointment of Pōtatau Te Wherowhero, the great great great grandfather of Te Arikinui Te Atairangikahu.

On 21 August 2006, prior to the departure of the waka bearing Dame Te Atairangikahu to her final resting place on Taupiri, the sacred mountain of Waikato, the queen's successor was announced and crowned at Turangawaewae. He is Tuheitia Paki, the eldest son of Te Atairangikahu. Mā te Atua e tiaki, e atawhai i te Kīngi Māori.

Nā reira, e Te Arikinui, haere, haere, haere. Haere ki Hawaiki nui, ki Hawaiki roa, ki Hawaiki pāmamao, ki te awhi o ōu tūpuna.

The new Māori King Tuheitia.

What of the future of the Kīngitanga?

There are still Treaty-related issues between Māori and the Crown to be resolved, and the Kīngitanga, which enjoys the respect of all political parties, will continue to be the central support for Tainui negotiations. Ways in which the Tainui people should benefit from Treaty settlements have to be developed and overseen and, inevitably, there will be intertribal differences to be settled.

After the national outpouring of grief and expressions of support for the Kīngitanga following the death of Te Arikinui Te Atairangikahu, it is difficult to imagine Maoridom or, indeed, Aotearoa as a nation without the Kīngitanga. Dame Te Ata made it her business to engage with other peoples of the Pacific and her efforts in this regard were reflected by the number of representatives of Pacific nations at her tangi. The state of countries within the Pacific has begun to concern the governments of New Zealand, Australia, and Pacific Rim nations as they watch Pacific governments grappling with problems of unemployment and interethnic disagreements. It could well be that the Kīngitanga has an expanding role to play in the Pacific.

THE MARAE

Entrance to Koroniti marae.

The marae is the heart of Māori culture. It is where all of the rituals are performed, agreements and disagreements hammered out, tribal policies promulgated and formalised, government policies affecting Māori are discussed, landcourts sit, and hui (meetings) on all manner of subjects are held. The marae is where tangihanga, the Māori funeral rituals, are held and it is this ritual that takes precedence over all other gatherings scheduled to be held at the marae.

The buildings on the marae contain tribal histories in their carvings, and pictures of tribal members both past and present will often adorn the walls of the wharenui, the main house.

These days we are seeing the marae used as they were in the days of the ancestors, in that they have reclaimed their rightful position to be the location of the specifically Māori institutions of learning, the wānanga.

So what is a marae?

In pre-European times Māori lived in fortified villages called pā, usually on a hill and located close to the coast or a river. However, when intertribal warfare ceased and the peace between Māori and European became a lasting peace, there was no need for Māori to continue to live in their fortified pā. They moved their villages to flat ground where it was more convenient to grow and tend crops and life in general was easier. As time went by more and more families moved into their own houses, located in settlements and villages alongside European settler families. The pā ceased to be the tribal place of residence and became instead the tribal meeting-place. The words pā and marae in modern Aotearoa are interchangeable.

Motukaraka marae, Hokianga.
Robert Key

The word marae has come to mean the collection of buildings and land within an area that is almost always defined by a fence or wall and, often, on one boundary by a river, lake or sea. Strictly speaking the marae is the area in front of the wharenui, the main house, and it is there that the formal speeches of welcome to manuhiri, visitors, are made and speeches of reply from the manuhiri to the tangata whenua (literally 'people of the land' but in this context 'hosts') are also made. This area is said to be the domain of Tūmatauenga, god of war, and as such, speeches here may pursue any theme – peaceful or otherwise. Speeches made

Whaikōrero.

within the walls of the wharenui, however, are governed by the precepts of Rongo, god of peace, and a spirit of goodwill is the pervading ethos of verbal exchanges made within what is, in fact, the manmade representation of an ancestor.

What happens at a marae?
Mārena (weddings), family celebrations, tangi, hui on all manner of subjects, and hosting of manuhiri from within and outside the tribal area. The marae is where the whānau (family), hapū (subtribe), and iwi gather to consider matters that affect them.

What buildings are located on a marae?

There is the main house, the wharenui, which is where the tangata whenua and the manuhiri conduct their meetings, and where they sleep. The wharenui may

Tāne-nui-a-Rangi wharenui at the University of Auckland. *Garry Brandon*

also be referred to as the wharetipuna or wharetupuna, ancestral house; wharepuni or wharemoe, sleeping house; wharehui, meeting house; or wharewhakairo, carved house.

The wharenui always bears a name which is, as often as not, the name of an ancestor of the marae on which it stands. There is also a generic name by which all wharenui are known: Tāne Whakapiripiri – Tāne who draws people closer together.

The carved figure on top of the front of the house is called the tekoteko. It is the ancestor's head, and the carved boards stretching out and down from the tekoteko are the ancestor's arms. Inside, there is a pole or board that runs the length of the whare ceiling called the tāhuhu and this is the ancestor's backbone. And coming off the tāhuhu and connecting with the carved figures around the walls are the ancestor's ribs, heke or wheke. The carved figures are representations of ancestors from the marae and, often, from other marae. They are called poupou.

It is usually on the courtyard in front of the wharenui that the formal speeches take part during a pōwhiri, welcome. It is this courtyard space that is the marae proper.

Interior of Tāne-nui-a-Rangi. *Garry Brandon*

The tūpāpaku and mourners reach the urupā.

Other buildings on the marae will include the wharekai (dining hall and kitchen), and a wharepaku (toilet) and wharehoroi (ablution block). In addition to all these buildings, there are sometimes accommodation blocks for kaumātua, tribal elders, located within a marae. Very often there is a whare karakia, church, situated either on or close by the marae, and always there is an urupā, cemetery or burial ground, usually located adjacent to the marae. It is here that the descendants of the marae are buried, thereby being united with and part of the ancestors of the marae. Very often the urupā will be situated on a hill that affords a beautiful view of the surrounding countryside.

The kawa, protocol, of the marae

View from Motukaraka urupā. *Robert Key*

The kawa of the marae differs in some respects within different tribal areas. The formation in which visitors enter the marae and whether or not women are permitted to speak on the marae proper are two such differences. Sometimes it is the men who head the visitors' entrance and other times it is the women. In most places the delivering of whaikōrero, formal speeches, on the marae is a male-only domain. A notable exception to this rule is within the tribal area of Ngāti Porou on the east coast of the North Island.

Hongi outside Tūrangawaewae marae.

So here is the procedure that you will follow when you are visiting a marae as part of an ope, party of manuhiri, visitors. This procedure is basically the same no matter what the occasion.

Te pōwhiri / The welcoming ceremony

You've arrived at the marae, and along with your fellow visitors you are standing outside the marae entrance. The leaders of your group will know the appropriate kawa for the marae so just follow their instructions as to whether it's men or women to head the entrance of the manuhiri. It is at this time that the koha is collected. Koha is a gift and it is the means whereby the manuhiri can contribute to the costs of the staging of whatever the occasion is that they are attending. There is usually no set amount to be paid for the koha collection, but do bear in mind the costs to the tangata whenua of organising the occasion and providing the hospitality to the manuhiri. In the old days koha would have consisted of food. Efforts would be made to koha special foods from the manuhiri area, foods that were not readily available in the tangata whenua area.

The group leaders will be in touch with the tangata whenua and at the appropriate time, when both sides are ready, a karanga, call of welcome, will ring out from inside the marae grounds. It's time to begin . . .

Te whakaekenga / The entrance onto the marae

The karanga signals the start of the pōwhiri, which means that your group will begin the whakaekenga, the entrance onto the marae. An important thing to be aware of is that the whakaekenga takes place in silence and that the manuhiri should be a tight-knit group – no stragglers. More marae are being declared 'smokefree zones', and it's not good form to smoke during the whakaekenga. There will usually be women among the visiting group who will answer the karanga from the tangata whenua with their own karanga, and the calls will go back and forth until your leader signals a halt to the forward movement of your ope, group. This halt is to enable everyone to silently remember the ancestors, including the recently departed. When manuhiri visit they form part of te hunga ora, the living. But just as the descendants of a marae gather, so do the ancestors, te hunga mate, the departed. And so the manuhiri bring their dead with them, so that not only will te hunga ora greet te hunga ora but also te hunga mate will greet te hunga mate.

After this pause in the manuhiri entrance onto the marae grounds, the tangata whenua will give a call or signal for the manuhiri to either whakatau mai or e noho. Both are your invitation to sit down. The people giving the whaikōrero on behalf of the manuhiri sit in the front row and the women who are supporting the speakers with waiata will sit behind them and then it's the rest, usually men in front of women. It's now time for . . .

The kaikaranga's call.

Ngā whaikōrero / The formal speeches

Once everyone is settled, the whaikōrero, formal speeches, and welcomes will begin. The speakers for the tangata whenua are seated on the paepae of the marae. The paepae is the seating especially set aside for the official speakers. Sometimes the paepae is the low wall that encloses the mahau, verandah, of the whare and sometimes it is seating especially placed for use as the paepae. This seating is usually located to the left of the wharenui. The word paepae can also be used to describe the group of kaikōrero, speakers, of either the tangata whenua or manuhiri. The kawa, protocol, for presentation of the whaikōrero varies, depending on the tribal affiliation of the tangata whenua. There are two main kawa that the whaikōrero process follows. One is called pāeke and the other tū mai tū atu.

Whaikōrero.

The pāeke kawa means that the tangata whenua will put forward all of their speakers first, leaving, however, one speaker to conclude the whaikōrero process after the speeches of the manuhiri have concluded. Whatever the kawa followed it is the tangata whenua who both commence and conclude the whaikōrero process. It is usual for the manuhiri to match the number of speakers to the number presented by the tangata whenua. As each kaikōrero concludes his speech there is a waiata performed by supporting members of the manuhiri and it is highly desirable that this group performing the waiata should include one or more women.

Where the tū mai tū atu kawa is observed the tangata whenua will begin the whaikōrero ritual. As each of their kaikōrero finishes their speech, the manuhiri will follow with one of their speakers. Again, waiata are performed at the conclusion of all speeches. When the last speech of the manuhiri has concluded and the supporting waiata performed, the speaker will then place the koha from the manuhiri on the marae. Sometimes the koha placement will be greeted by a karanga from one of the tangata whenua kaikaranga, who may also collect the koha. At other times the tangata whenua may get their last speaker to collect the koha after his whaikōrero and waiata have concluded. This effectively signals an end of the whaikōrero process – which means that it is time for the manuhiri and tangata whenua to greet one another one to one. The tangata whenua will signal the manuhiri that they are now ready for their manuhiri to come forward and be greeted by all the tangata whenua at the marae.

You just follow the person in front of you as your ope advances single file over to the tangata whenua, who will be lined up waiting to welcome you with a harirū, handshake, or hongi, or kihi, kiss on the cheek, or even all three.

How to hongi

The hongi is the Māori greeting. Nose pressed against nose. Often, but not always, forehead against forehead, always the handshake, harirū, often your non-shaking hand on your opposite's shoulder, and either one or two presses of the noses. The eyes should be closed throughout the entire interface. The number and length of the nose presses is at the discretion of your host. Just follow them. Go with the flow. At the conclusion of the hongi it is good form to say 'Tēnā koe' or 'Kia ora'.

Hongi.

You will often see the hongi at a hāngi, and always at a marae. These days the hongi is increasingly seen at any social occasion attended by Māori, so it is as well to be prepared to take part in the hongi.

If this is your first visit to this marae, your official status prior to your one-to-one welcome from the tangata whenua is that of waewae tapu, a first-timer. Once this physical affirmation of the welcomes and greetings as expressed in the mihi, spoken welcome, and whaikōrero is finished, you are deemed to be a member of the tangata whenua for the duration of your visit. You are now free to socialise with your friends and the tangata whenua.

Whatever your reason for visiting the marae there will be a programme to be followed so make sure you know what's scheduled and observe things accordingly. It's quite likely that if your pōwhiri took place mid-morning, then you will be invited to partake of a kapu tī, a cup of tea, and/or morning tea or kai, lunch, in the wharekai. This invitation is issued by way of the ringing of a bell. Whether it's the kapu tī or kai, there are a few simple things to remember about the kawa, etiquette of the wharekai . . .

Te wharekai / dining hall

It is good manners to answer the call of the bell promptly. Unlike the removal of footwear rule that applies in the wharenui, shoes are usually worn inside the wharekai. However, if your shoes are muddy or you see that people have removed their shoes before entering the wharekai, then it's a good idea for you to follow suit and remove yours.

Seating in the wharekai usually starts from the end nearest the kitchen and works back towards the entrance. It's important for the smooth flow of things that all seats in rows be filled before another row is started. The tables will be filled one by one and, rather than try and sit with particular people, just sit wherever the next available seat is. This all helps maintain a good flow of diners, and you have the opportunity to meet new people. Do not linger over your kai as there are plenty of people to be fed and the tangata whenua cannot eat or clean up until all the manuhiri have been fed.

Wait for a karakia, grace, to be said before eating or drinking.

Do not sit on the tables.

Should you be at the marae for more than one meal it is nice to help with the work in the kitchen. In doing this you will be joining ngā ringawera, literally the 'hot-handed ones', who work tirelessly in the kitchens during gatherings on the marae.

It's common for the poroporoaki, farewell speeches, to take place in the wharekai after the final meal and it's good form to be prepared to say a few words of appreciation in Māori at that time. You'll find a short speech which you can use for such occasions at the end of this chapter. As always, just go with the flow, and you will know when the time is right for you to take to your feet and say your piece. Don't forget to thank your hosts and ngā ringawera.

In the event that you are staying overnight at the marae here are some things to remember.

The marae provides mattresses, pillows, and sheets and you bring the rest.

Leave your sleeping things outside the marae until after the pōwhiri.

All footwear is to be removed before entering the wharenui. However, slippers may be worn while inside.

There are sleeping areas set aside for both the tangata whenua and manuhiri. It is usually to the left of the whatitoka, doorway, that the tangata whenua sleep and to the right for the manuhiri. The positions immediately to right and left of the doorway and under the window are often reserved for kaumātua of both hosts and visitors, so when you are placing your bedding in the wharenui it's a good idea to leave these spaces free.

During both evening and daytime discussions inside the wharenui people will sit on the mattresses, so remember to keep your space tidy and refrain from sitting on the pillows. The reason for this prohibition is that the head is the most tapu part of the body and it should not come into contact with a pillow which has been sat on.

Tangihanga

Should you be attending a tangi, there are one or two additional things for you to be aware of. You will notice that many of the women present and some of the men have their heads wrapped in greenery. This is a sign of mourning and kawakawa leaves are widely used for this purpose.

Mourners wearing garlands of greenery.

The tūpāpaku, body of the departed one, lies in an open casket on the mahau, verandah of the wharenui, and is surrounded by the whānau pani, the bereaved family.

After the burial the people present are in a tapu state and, in order to remove the tapu, your hands need to be washed. Many marae will have a container of water situated outside the urupā, cemetery, for this purpose.

Urupā at Parihaka.

Once the burial is done it is time to return to the marae for the hākari, feast, which always concludes the tangi.

In the next chapter you will see how the hākari is cooked.

He mihi mōu / A greetings speech for you

As in all things Māori there are tikanga, procedures and forms, to be observed in the presentation of mihi and whaikōrero. In some aspects the words mihi and whaikōrero are interchangeable. Mihi are speeches of greeting, welcome and appreciation. Whaikōrero contain mihi but they also have other kaupapa, themes and plots.

And so what follows is a mihi you could use to introduce yourself in the wharenui during the evening mihimihi sessions or those preceding the official business of your particular hui.

Tihei mauri ora!	Literally 'the breath of life'.
E te whare e tū nei	To you the house that stands here
Tēnā koe	Greetings
E te marae e takoto nei	And to you the marae that lies here
Tēnā koe	Greetings
E ngā mate o tēnei marae	To the departed ones of this marae
Me ngā marae o te motu	And those of all the marae of the nation
Haere, haere, haere.	Go swiftly to your resting place.
Ko Wiremu taku ingoa	My name is William
Nō Ākarana au.	I am from Auckland.
Kei te nui taku mihi	Great are my greetings
Ki a koutou, ngā tāngata whenua	To you my hosts
Mō ōu koutou manaakitanga	For your hospitality
Ki a mātou.	To us.

Nā reira	And so
Tēnā koutou, tēnā koutou,	
Tēnā tātou katoa.	Greetings to you one and all.

Should you be making a speech during the poroporoaki, farewell, in the wharekai, you could add in a little mihi to ngā ringawera.

So your last section could go thus . . .

Kei te nui taku mihi	
Ki a koutou ngā tāngata whenua	
Me koutou hoki ngā ringawera	And also to you, ngā ringawera
Aha te reka o te kai!	Such delicious food!
Mō ōu koutou manaakitanga	
Ki a mātou	
Nā reira,	
Tēnā koutou, tēnā koutou,	
Tēnā tātou katoa.	

THE HĀNGI

The hāngi is the earth oven used by Māori to cook their food. These days it has also come to mean the cooked food that has come out of the hāngi.

Hāngi requirements

1. At least a metre of mānuka (teatree). Other wood will do the job but mānuka is the preferred choice.
2. A large clean cotton sheet (not bed linen) to cover the food.
3. Enough sacking, the old-fashioned sort, to put three layers over the sheet.
4. At least one shovel.
5. Hāngi stones. These aren't easy to find but you will sometimes find them for sale in the classified ads. Volcanic stones or riverstones are what you're after, and you will need someone who knows how to recognise them if you decide to be totally original. Steel bars are sometimes used in place of, or as well as, stones.

Placing the food in the hāngi.

6. Steel-mesh baskets to place food in.
7. Food: meat (can be any sort and in any combination), vegetables (peeled potatoes, kūmara, onions, pumpkin, marrow), stuffing, steamed puddings – particularly nice done in the hāngi.

Procedure

Wet the sacks and leave them soaking (best left to soak overnight) while you do the following:

1. Usually the men's job is to prepare the fire and the women's to prepare the food. Whatever the division of labour, the food needs to be ready to go into the hāngi at the appropriate time.
2. Dig a dish-like pit about 1–1.5 m in diameter and maybe. 25 m deep. Keep the dirt piled up, as you'll need it later.
3. Prepare the fire. Stack the wood lattice-like so that it will collapse inwards.
4. Put the stones on top of the wood.
5. Light the fire and let it burn until all the wood has burned and the stones have fallen into the pit – about 1–1.5 hours . . . certainly time to wet the whistle.
6. Remove all ashes and any remaining unburned wood from the pit. Some people leave some still-burning wood in as they like the resulting smoky taste of the food. Temporarily remove the stones. You will need shovels for this task.
7. Give the pit floor a good whack with a wet sack.
8. Put the stones back in the pit and give them a good whack with the sack. The sack-whack is to get rid of any remaining ash.
9. Place the food in the baskets, which should already be prepared, with the slowest cooking food at the bottom. The baskets should be lined with tinfoil and that lined with cabbage leaves.
10. Pour about half a bucket of water on the stones and then quickly place the baskets on the stones.

11. Cover the baskets with the cotton sheet and extend the sheet out to the perimeter of the pit.

12. Cover the sheet with sacking . . . moving at top speed at this stage.

13. Cover the sacking with the dirt you dug from the pit, working from the bottom up.

14. Once the sacking is totally covered, you will need to stay on duty for an hour to shovel dirt over the outlets that the steam inevitably finds.

The hāngi will take about three hours to cook so you've plenty of time to prepare the venue for the upcoming feasting.

After three hours, uncover the sacking and remove it and the cotton cover. Make sure you've got heat-resistant gloves to enable you to remove the baskets of food to the table where they can be served. Put the dirt back into the pit (having removed the stones) and . . . Bob's your uncle.

Enjoy your hāngi kai!

You should be aware that there is another widely used method of preparing the hāngi. The difference to the one outlined above is this.

The hāngi is opened.

Instead of lighting the fire to heat the stones over the pit, light a fire adjacent to the pit and heat the stones. Once the fire has burnt down and the stones are properly heated, transfer the stones to the pit. This, of course, makes for a cleaner hāngi, as you don't have to worry about removing ash from the pit before you place the food baskets over the stones.

66

MĀORI ARTS

Māori arts are the means of recording tribal history, acknowledging the spiritual world, and illustrating whakapapa. Spiritual world symbols are contained in the artforms of whakairo (carving), raranga (weaving) and moko (tattoo).

Whakairo / carving

While pounamu, greenstone, came to be a taonga of the Māori through a battle that raged across the breadth of Te Moana nui a Kiwa, the Pacific Ocean, whakairo was obtained only after a god's house was plundered.

Ruatepupuke visited Tangaroa's whare beneath the sea and there observed that the poupou, the supporting boards of the whare walls, were carved – unlike those of the whare of his homeland, which were painted. Not only that, the poupou, which are human figures, could speak!

Ruatepupuke set fire to Tangaroa's whare and stole some of the pou, the carved posts, outside to take back to his world. Unfortunately the pou lost the ability to speak. But their very presence was a detailed guide to would-be tohunga whakairo, master carvers.

Kaiwhakairo (carvers) at work.

Carved panel inside Tāne-nui-a-Rangi. *Garry Brandon*

Carving in stone.

Whare today are, with some exceptions, carved works of art. Those that are not carved have a beauty of their own when they are painted with traditional figures and forms. The names of them and the carving and weaving in the whare contain the history of the iwi that belong to the whare.

The whare whakairo, carved houses, are decorated with carved amo (bargeboards), and poupou. At the apex of the amo on the outside of the whare is the tekoteko, a carved figure or head. The bases of the supporting ridgepole are poupou, which are round, and often with the whole circumference carved.

Trees such as kauri were easily split and free of knots. Pounamu and other fine-grained rock made excellent tools for the carver. Of course, modern times demand modern tools and the carvers of today use steel chisels.

Carvings are usually painted with kōkōwai, red ochre – to the romantics, the earthen result of Papatūānuku's tears at being separated from her lover Ranginui. To the more analytical, kōkōwai consists of a special clay that has a high iron oxide content and is mixed with shark oil. This produces a thick red paint.

There are some forms that recur in the various forms of Māori art. Some examples follow below.

The koru – the unfolding fern frond – which is a common form in whakairo – illustrates the life cycle of man. The different forms of the koru trace the life cycle from the time in the womb to the time of old age.

The manaia is the spirit that each person has. It is protective of its human subject and, at the appointed time, the manaia will guide the spirit of the deceased human to the departure place for the spirit world. The carved form of the manaia usually has three fingers representing birth, life and death, plus the head of a bird which symbolises flight. Sometimes it will have a fourth finger representing the afterlife. It is also believed by some that the three fingers represent the three kete of knowledge.

Tiki was the personification of primeval man and also represents the male organ te ure, the penis. It is said that it was through Tiki that the life-giving waters of the heavens and the waters of the deep sea entered the womb of Hineahuone – who was the first person born into the world – and created the people of the earth.

The three kete of knowledge in Tāne-nui-a-Rangi.
Gary Brandon

Carved wooden tiki are very obviously male, while the pounamu (greenstone) carved figures that are worn as pendants and are called heitiki, are generally female forms. The heitiki are taonga, treasured possessions of Māori and they are also very popular with people of all races who want something that identifies with things Māori.

The art of whakairo is now thriving, although in 1963 the government felt compelled to pass legislation designed to preserve whakairo in all its forms. Out of this came the New Zealand Maori Arts and Crafts Institute, which involved the setting up of Te Wānanga Whakairo, the carving school, and Te Rito, the weaving school. The institute is situated at Te Puia Springs in Rotorua and is the living embodiment of much of Māori culture. There are a variety of cultural performances and demonstrations, which tourists and the general public are welcome to attend. Enquiries can be directed through the website www.nzmaori.co.nz.

One branch of whakairo that largely disappeared during the early and mid

A performer receives a temporary moko.

twentieth century is tā moko, tattoo. However, in the late twentieth century and into the new millennium tā moko has made a steady resurgence.

Tā moko is a language that records for all to see the tribal affiliation, rank, status and occupation of the bearer of the moko. For men the main areas of the body to be tattooed are the face and buttocks, while for women the areas are lips and chin. Other areas of the body may also be tattooed such as the thighs, back, and lower legs.

The traditional process of applying tā moko is both long and painful. The skin is cut with a chisel and mallet and pigment made with charcoal is rubbed into the cut grooves of the skin. There are a number of patterns used, with spiral patterns forming the basis of the overall design.

Raranga / weaving

Māori did not have a written language until after the arrival of the missionaries. However, along with the oral histories passed between generations, much of the tribal histories and legends were permanently recorded for all to refer to in the carving and weaving of the various iwi.

Just as carving was a gift from the gods, so was weaving. The importance of weaving to Polynesia generally is emphasised by the tale of Tāne when he undertook his quest to gain the knowledge that would be crucial to the survival of the trees, plants and people that he had created. That knowledge was held by the supreme deity Io in three woven kete, baskets – which are often represented in whakairo.

Raranga is one of the taonga of Hineteiwaiwa, who is the female personification of the marama, moon. The craft was, however, introduced to the Māori by another woman from the spirit world called Niwareka, who visited the human world and married Mataora. At some point Niwareka left her husband and returned to Rarohenga, the underworld, to which Mataora then journeyed in search of his wife. While in Rarohenga, Mataora learned the art of moko, which is another of the whakairo arts.

Niwareka reconciled with Mataora and returned to earth, bringing with her Rangihaupapa, which was a woven cloak that became the model for all such cloaks.

Most raranga was done using harakeke, flax fibre, which was sometimes dyed. There were no looms involved in the process. The first horizontal fibres were attached to poles in the ground and the vertical fibres were then attached to the lead horizontal ones. The garment was formed or woven by inserting the horizontal fibres into the vertical ones.

Raranga could be a very time-consuming activity, with cloaks often taking months to complete. It is also a tradition that the first article woven by a student of raranga is to be gifted.

Raranga creations include korowai (cloaks), kete (baskets), whāriki (mats) and, increasingly these days, novelty-type creations such as flowers.

A kete raranga.

POUNAMU
GREENSTONE

Pounamu is a highly prized taonga of Māori. And like all taonga, it was not easily obtained. It came to Aotearoa only after an epic battle that crossed oceans.

Poutini was the rangatira of the Pounamu iwi, which originally lived in Hawaiki. The Pounamu iwi possessed magical powers that enabled them to turn themselves into fish – an attribute that would prove very handy when they were forced to flee their attackers – and from fish back into humans.

Poutini wanted his people to be able to occupy particular coastal waters off Hawaiki, and he sought the agreement of Tutunui, rangatira of the Whale iwi. Tutunui would not agree to Poutini's plans, and eventually war broke out – not between the iwi of Poutini and Tutunui, but between the Pounamu and their greatest enemy, the Hōanga (sandstone) iwi, whose aid Tutunui enlisted. The Hōanga iwi prevailed over the Pounamu, who were forced to flee their Hawaiki homeland. Taking the form of fish, they beat a fast watery retreat, punctuated by many battles along the way.

Eventually the well travelled Pounamu reached the Arahura River on the west coast of Te Waka a Māui, another name for the South Island of Aotearoa. With the Hōanga snapping at their tails, the Pounamu came to a waterfall in the river and darted behind it. The shoals of their enemy swept past. Safe at last!

Poutini and his iwi settled about the Arahura River, while others adopted homes elsewhere on the West Coast, which even today is called Te Tai Poutini – the greenstone sea. The whole of Te Waka a Māui came to be known as Te Waipounamu – greenstone waters.

There are several different types of pounamu with colours ranging from black to white. It was and still is highly prized. Pounamu is rare – it is only found in remote areas of the West Coast – and is highly valuable. It is used only for special taonga such as tiki (pendants), mere (clubs) and toki (adzes).

The fashioning of pounamu taonga was a long and laborious task. It was cut to size by rubbing it with water and sandstone. After it had been shaped and ground it was polish-finished by rubbing it against the skin – something which would take months, even years.

There is a whakataukī that illustrates the prized nature of pounamu:

He iti, he pounamu.
It might be small but it is very special.
(This may be heard when a small gift or koha is given.)

POI

Poi.

The poi – which you will often see when Māori perform their action songs – is a little ball on the end of a piece of string. It is used with great effect to amplify, and give clarification to, the words and meanings of songs. These songs are called haka poi or waiata poi and, like haka, they are the vehicles for composers to present their points of view on any subject to the public. In haka poi the use of the poi replaces the various moves and actions that are part of haka and waiata-ā-ringa, action songs.

Unlike haka and waiata-ā-ringa, the poi is unique to New Zealand. The origin of the poi is clouded in mysticism but the traditional materials used in the making of it are traceable to the gods. Tānemahuta, god of the forest, mated with Hineteropū, who is the personification of swamp, and the fruit of their union was raupō (bulrush) which is used to make the poi ball. Tānemahuta also mated with Pakoti and the result of that union was a special species of harakeke (flax), which is plaited into a rope and used to make the taura (handle) of the poi.

The poi is a work of art. The making of a poi is a clearly defined process which takes time and discipline, starting with the workers reciting the appropriate karakia and then entering the swamp to collect the raupō. Of course, as technology has continued to provide new textiles, the materials used to make poi have also evolved. Modern materials include foam rubber, paper, plastic, cotton and wool.

A waiata-ā-ringa

The main function of the poi is to help the composer of the waiata to get their message across to the people watching the performance of the haka poi. It is the way in which the poi communicates that takes the exponents of poi a great deal of time to learn and master. There are a whole range of 'classic' poi manoeuvres to be learned as a base, to which new movements are continually added. Just as with haka, the poi is an instrument that requires the involvement of the whole body in order for the ultimate effects to be realised. Pūkana (the dilating of the eyes), feet-stamping, dance steps, changing body stances and, of course, the correct manipulation of the wrist, fingers and hands, are all part of the performance of the poi.

And there is not just one poi that needs to be mastered. There is the poi waeroa or poi awe, the long poi. The poi kōkau, the short poi. The poi takirua, the double short poi, and the poi takitahi or single short poi. There is also the poi piu which is like a mini piupiu, grass skirt, with a rope handle. Māori have entertained tourists for many years with their poi performances, and out of the enthusiastic receptions accorded the performers, was born the mini-poi, which was specifically created as a souvenir for tourists.

The haka poi are sometimes used in ceremonial pōwhiri to distinguished visitors, and their future presence within Māoritanga is assured by the biennial Māori performing arts festival Te Matatini.

Apart from the beauty and grace of the haka poi there were other practical benefits for the poi exponents, of whom most are women. Learning the various

Dalvanius Prime at the Gluepot,
Ponsonby. *Graham Hooper*

manoeuvres not only provided excellent exercises in making the body flexible, it instilled discipline: exponents must be capable multi-taskers, able to keep in time with the haka and switch manoeuvres without batting an eyelid.

And so today you are able to attend performances of haka poi in many of the tourist hotels throughout the country, especially in and around Rotorua, where haka poi continues to evolve, with the addition of lighting effects and fire serving to embellish the beauty of the poi.

In the mid 1980s, two of Maoridom's famous composers, Ngoi Pewhairangi of Ngāti Porou and Dalvanius Prime of Ngā Rauru and Ngāti Ruanui, composed a haka poi and combined it with a pop music beat of the day to achieve a number one radio hit with 'Poi e' – in spite of staunch resistance from the radio networks of the day to providing the haka poi with airplay. But that's another tale. It was, however, the fusion of the traditional with the contemporary that exposed poi to a huge market, with 'Poi e' becoming a stage show that was performed throughout the world. So stand by for the hip-hop haka poi!

WHAIWHAI
HUNTING

Fish, seafood and birds formed important parts of the Māori diet. The oceans and waterways yielded an abundant supply of food to the fishermen who had a finely developed array of tools to harvest Tangaroa's offspring.

Fishing hooks were made of bone, wood, shell, or stone. Nets were made from harakeke, flax and tī rākau, cabbage-tree leaves. In addition, there were spears, dredges, and baskets. As with all activities of the Maori, fishing was carried out in accordance with the tides and the phases of the moon. The first catch was given back to Tangaroa as an offering and to assure the continued abundance of the species.

Until Captain Cook released pigs in Aotearoa, there were no large animals that could be hunted for food. The moa, a giant flightless bird, had been hunted to extinction by the time of the arrival of the European. There were plenty of birds, though, including the kiwi. Māori used spears, snares, decoys and nets to ensure a plentiful supply of food for the whanau.

If stocks of a particular species of birds or fish were becoming depleted, a rāhui would be placed on that species, or over a fishing ground, until it had recovered.

The pigs released by Captain Cook in 1769 adopted their new abode with enthusiasm, and quickly became a preferred food of Māori. These wild pigs, often referred to as 'Captain Cookers', are still keenly hunted by both Māori and Pākehā alike.

If you would like to participate in a pig-hunting expedition or go on a fishing trip escorted by Māori guides, visit www.maoriexperienz.co.nz or some of the other websites listed at the end of this book.

Inanga (whitebait).

PĀKANGA AND PATU
BATTLES AND WEAPONS

Mā te wahine me te whenua e ngaro ai te tangata. It is for women and land that men will die.

Māori loved to fight, and fighting was an artform that males were schooled in from a very early age. Tūmatauenga is god of war, and men and warriors were taught ritual chants and karakia to enlist his aid.

The reasons for war were many as wrongs and resentments would be harboured for long periods – often over generations. And it was incumbent on a tribe to exact utu, revenge for wrongs, no matter how long ago they occurred.

Before the arrival of Europeans, Aotearoa was inhabited by many different hapū and iwi who thought of themselves as nation states, each with their clearly defined boundaries. These nations were in areas that contained the various whanau, hapū and iwi, all of whom traced to the same waka. However, the ties of whakapapa notwithstanding, it was common for hapū to attack hapū.

Warrior with patu outside a fortified pā.

Warrior with taiaha.

Before the musket was introduced there were three types of weapon used in warfare – striking, thrusting and throwing weapons.

The taiaha, which is a hardwood weapon about 2 metres long, was used for both striking and thrusting.

The mere could also be used for both striking and thrusting. The mere pounamu was the most prized of the handheld clubs. It was easily concealed, being about 40 cm long and around 8 cm wide. Most warriors would employ the mere for the really close action and the taiaha for the not-quite-so-close encounters.

The wero is a spear, of which there were different types. The short wero, about 2 metres long, was used both as a handheld spear (not thrown) and a staff. Other much longer wero would be used from behind a palisade, where their length made them very useful in stopping an attacker before he actually got to the pā walls.

And so it was survival of the fittest. Until the musket arrived.

The musket had a devastating effect on tribes that did not possess this new weapon. It was introduced by traders to the northern tribes in the early 1800s and they made much of their monopoly. The muskets gradually became more evenly distributed, assisted in part by traders who put the word out that they would accept tattooed heads as barter for their weapons.

The Land Wars, which were accompanied by religious movement suppression campaigns, were waged from the mid 1840s though until the 1880s, although the last shot between the parties was not fired until 1916 at Maungapōhatu, the home of the religious movement of the prophet Rua Kenana. These wars enveloped the whole country, although not all iwi fought against the Crown. In fact a number supported and fought alongside the colonial troops. Such support however, was no guarantee that their lands would not be seized!

RONGOĀ MĀORI
HEALING, PLANTS

The Maori concept of healing is holistic and involves both the spiritual and physical realms, which in turn invoke the concepts of tapu and noa, the very basis of Maori society. Tapu is a state of ritual or sacred restriction, which can apply to people or things. In order to remove the tapu and apply a state of noa or non-tapu, there are certain rituals and karakia which must be performed or recited to placate the offended spirit.

The physical healing elements were those properties held by plants and herbs which were harnessed by the tohunga. To the Māori, the plants were living beings originating from the same gods as themselves, and Tāne, god of the forest, or Rongo, god of cultivated plants, had to be placated when their offpsring were required for rongoā, healing purposes.

The tohunga were experts in mythology, history, astronomy, medicine and makutu (witchcraft). Admission to the various whare wānanga that taught these disciplines was restricted by the potential tohunga's standing within the tribe, and that was determined by birth and mana. There was no written language, so it was a huge undertaking to learn not only the medicinal properties of plants, but also the correct karakia for the rongoā to be effective. In addition to this, tohunga learnt how to physically treat broken bones, war wounds, respiratory ailments, and a whole range of other ills.

Early European visitors remarked that the Māori enjoyed excellent health. But scourges brought by the whalers, traders, and colonists – such as measles, influenza, venereal diseases, typhoid – wrought devastation on the Māori. Such was the effect of the imported diseases that, combined with the general malaise of colonisation, some officials predicted that the Māori race was headed for extinction. But as with te reo, and Māori culture generally, te rongoā Māori has enjoyed a resurgence, particularly since the 1970s.

Government health agencies are incorporating te rongoā Māori into the treatment of Māori, and the tohunga continues to play an important role in maintaining the health of the people.

> E kore au e ngaro he kākano nō Rai'ātea.
> I will never disappear, the seed from Rai'ātea.

At the time of writing there is a claim before the Waitangi Tribunal that seeks to protect the intellectual property rights of the Māori over plants and their healing qualities.

Whāu leaves were used to treat wounds.

TOURIST ACTIVITIES WEBSITES

www.Maoriexperienz.co.nz

The excellent website of a company owned by Māori involved in tourism. Has links to regional Māori tourism organisations.

www.whalewatch.co.nz

This is the website for the award-winning whale-watching operation of the Ngāi Tahu iwi of the South Island, i.e. Te Waka a Māui.

www.onenz.co.nz

Excellent general information, including Māori-based activities, for travellers.

www.nzescape.com

Another excellent general information website.

www.whanganuiriver.co.nz

'I am the river and the river is me.' Check out this website of the indigenous iwi of the Whanganui River.

www.navigatortours.co.nz

Indigenous tours and activities.

www.maorifood.com

Not just how to hāngi – although that is well covered. Indigenous food tours, recipes featuring indigenous herbs, virtual shop – it is all on this site of one of Aotearoa's most acclaimed chefs.

www.tohuwines.co.nz

The first Māori owned and operated winery and recipient of many awards.

www.nzmaori. co.nz

The website lists many cultural activities in the Rotorua area, including the NZ Arts and Crafts Institute at Te Puia Springs.

www.tematatini.org.nz

Details of the biennial Māori performing arts festival and the Māori music awards are found on this website.

BIBLIOGRAPHY

Armstrong, Alan, *Maori Games and Haka* new edition, Reed, Auckland, 2005.

Best, Elsdon *The Maori As He Was: A brief account of Life as it was Pre-European Days*

Harawira, Wena Te Kawa o te Marae –(Reed 1997. 2000)

Huata, Ngamoni, *The Rhythm and Life of Poi*, Harper Collins, Auckland, 2000.

Karetu, T.S., *Haka The Dance of a Noble People*, Reed, Auckland, 1993.

King, Michael, *Nga Iwi o Te Motu: 1000 years of Maori History*, Reed, Auckland, 2003.

Kururangi, Mere, *Weaving: The Arts of the Maori Instructional Booklet*, Art and Crafts
    Branch, Department of Education, Wellington, 1976.

Leather, Kay & Richard Hall, *Tatai Arorangi Maori Astronomy: Work of the Gods*, Viking
    Sevenseas, Wellington, 2004.

Mead, Hirini Moko & Neil Grove, Ngaa Peepeha a Ngaa Tiipuna, Victoria University Press,
    Wellington, 2001.

Orange, Claudia, *An Illustrated History of The Treaty of Waitangi*, Bridget Williams
    Books, Wellington, 2004.

——, *The Story of a Treaty*, Bridget Williams Books, Wellington, 2000.

Reed, A.W., *Maori Placenames and Their Meanings*, A.H.& A.W. Reed, Wellington, 1959.

——, revised by Buddy Mikaere, *Taonga Tuku Iho: Illustrated Encyclopedia of
    Traditional Maori Life*, Reed, Auckland, 2002.

Riley, Murdoch, *Maori Healing and Herbal*, Viking Sevenseas, Wellington, 2003.

Stafford, Don, *Introducing Maori Culture*, Reed, Auckland, 2001.

——, *Tangata Whenua: The World of the Maori*, Reed, Auckland, 2005.

Tauroa, Hiwi & Pat, *Te Marae: A Guide to Customs and Protocol*, Reed, Auckland, 2004.

Te Ohorere raua ko Wiiremu Kaa (nga etita), *Nga Korero a Reweti Kohere Maa*, Victoria
    University Press, Wellington, 1994.

Wepa, Matthew Eru, *Symbols of the Maori World*, revised edition, self-published,
    Rotorua.

Williams, P.M., *Te Rongoa Maori. Maori Medicine*, Reed, Auckland, 1996.

Winitana, Chris, *Legends of Aotearoa*, HarperCollins, Auckland, 2001.